DANGEROUS ANIMALS OF THE WORLD

Book for Kids

WONDERFUL WORLD OF ANIMALS BOOK 3

JACK LEWIS

Dangerous Animals of the World Book for Kids
Wonderful World of Animals Book 3
Copyright © 2022 by Starry Dreamer Publishing

For information contact:
Starry Dreamer Publishing LLC
1603 Capitol Ave. Suite 310 A377
Cheyenne, Wyoming 82001
starrydreamerpub@gmail.com

Written by Jack Lewis
Photo Credits: All images contained herein are used under license from Shutterstock.com and Pixabay.com (See Index for complete list)
Front Cover Photo Credits:
Ramon Carretero, Rudi Hulshof, Thorsten Spoerlein, J. Natayo/Shutterstock
Back Cover Photo Credits:
Patrick K. Campbell, David Havel, Three Alienz/Shutterstock

ISBN: 978-1-952328-69-5 (Hardcover) 978-1-952328-66-4 (Paperback) 978-1-952328-70-1 (Ebook)
Library of Congress Cataloging-in-Publication Data is available
10 9 8 7 6 5 4 3 2 1
First Edition: June 2022

STARRY DREAMER PUBLISHING

INDIAN SAW-SCALED VIPER
The Middle East and Central Asia

FIERCE FACT:
THESE VIPERS WILL FORM A COIL AND RUB THEIR SCALES TOGETHER TO MAKE A SIZZLING SOUND IF THEY FEEL THREATENED!

The Indian saw-scaled viper is extremely aggressive and is one of the four deadliest snakes in India. It is responsible for a huge number of snakebite cases and deaths each year.

KOMODO DRAGON
Indonesia's Lesser Sunda Islands

Komodo dragons are the dominant predators in their habitats and will eat almost anything they find, including deer, water buffalo, pigs, other Komodo dragons, and even humans! If an animal escapes the jaws of the dragon, the Komodo will patiently follow their prey for miles until it dies.

WHY ARE DANGEROUS ANIMALS IMPORTANT?

Dangerous animals play important roles in their ecosystems. Many of them use their natural "weapons" to defend themselves or hunt for food. Often these animals are predators and help keep other animal species from becoming too overpopulated, and sometimes they serve as an important food source for other creatures.

Amazingly, the venoms and poisons from dangerous animals are frequently used in medical research to create new medicines! Unfortunately, due to climate change, over-hunting, and habitat destruction, many special creatures are on the brink of extinction.

WHAT SHOULD I DO IF I ENCOUNTER AN ANIMAL IN THE WILD?

Exploring nature is a wonderful and exciting adventure! Whether you're swimming in a lake or an ocean, hiking through the woods, or climbing a mountain, it is always a good idea to keep your distance from any wild animals you may meet along the way. Remember, most animals in nature just want to be left alone, so never try and pet or feed a wild animal.

Here are a few good ideas to stay safe while you're exploring the great outdoors:

• **Always travel with another person** – Bring a friend or family member with you when you're exploring nature. You not only get to share the fun of the experience, but you'll also have someone with you if an emergency occurs.

• **Learn about the wildlife in the area** – Educate yourself and learn about what animals and insects you may encounter on your outdoor adventure and how to avoid any that might be dangerous.

• **Leave wild animals alone** – Never try and feed or pet an animal you meet in nature. (Save your treats and cuddles for your pets at home!)

• **Pay attention** – Whenever you're in nature, pay attention to what you're doing and what is around you. Not only will it help keep you safe, but also you won't miss out on seeing something cool!

• **Insect Repellant** – In areas with dangerous insects, it is wise to wear insect repellant to keep them away!

• **Keep your distance** – If you meet a wild animal and it approaches you, stay calm and don't run. Face the animal and slowly back away from it. Make a lot of noise and shout while you get as far away from it as you can.

ELECTRIC EEL
South America

FIERCE FACT:
AN ELECTRIC EEL CAN DELIVER A SHOCK POWERFUL ENOUGH TO KNOCK DOWN A FULL-GROWN HORSE!

These "shocking" creatures aren't really eels but are related to carps and catfish. A mature electric eel can measure over 8 feet long. They have 6,000 special cells in their body that act like tiny batteries. Electric eels can deliver a powerful 600-volt zap!

CAPE BUFFALO
Africa

FIERCE FACT:

CAPE BUFFALO ARE REPORTED TO KILL MORE HUNTERS ON THE AFRICAN CONTINENT THAN ANY OTHER CREATURE!

The Cape buffalo is one of four subspecies of African buffalo. They are large, hardy creatures that can survive in many different habitats. These buffalo have massive horns and are a dangerous mix of powerful, unpredictable, and grumpy.

CONE SNAIL
Indo-Pacific Reefs

FIERCE FACT:
THERE IS NO EXISTING ANTIVENOM OR ANTIDOTE FOR THIS SNAIL'S TOXIN. YIKES!

This deadly snail has venom so powerful it can paralyze another animal instantly. Believe it or not, proteins from the cone snail's venom are used to create a painkilling medicine 1,000 times more potent than morphine.

BROWN RECLUSE
The U.S. and Mexico

SEVERE REACTIONS TO THIS SPIDER'S BITE CAN LEAD TO A "VOLCANO LESION"— AN OPEN WOUND THAT CAN BE AS LARGE AS A HUMAN HAND!

This venomous spider has one terrible bite! The brown recluse gets its name from its color and shy nature. It generally avoids humans but can deliver a nasty, dangerous bite if disturbed.

RUSSELL'S VIPER
South Asia

FIERCE FACT:
EVEN IF A PERSON IS LUCKY ENOUGH TO SURVIVE AN ATTACK FROM THIS VIPER, THEY MAY STILL EXPERIENCE SEVERE PAIN FOR UP TO FOUR WEEKS!

The Russell's viper is another one of the four most dangerous snakes on the Indian subcontinent. Their large nostrils are believed to help them track their prey by detecting body heat.

GRIZZLY BEAR
North America

The grizzly bear is an enormous, powerful mammal. Able to run up to 30 miles per hour, stand eight feet tall, and weigh up to 900 pounds, this impressive bear is one you never want to meet close-up in the wild! Sadly, these impressive animals are an endangered species.

FIERCE FACT:
IN ALASKA, YOU MIGHT SPOT A HYBRID BEAR KNOWN AS THE "PIZZLY BEAR," A STRANGE CROSS BETWEEN GRIZZLIES AND POLAR BEARS!

MAN O' WAR

Oceans Across the World

FIERCE FACT:

THE TENTACLES OF THE MAN O' WAR CAN STRETCH UP TO 100 FEET AND STILL STING EVEN IF IT IS DEAD!

The Portuguese man o' war can be found in warm tropical waters worldwide. It looks like a jellyfish, but it is an animal called a "siphonophore." Although it rarely kills, the sting of the man o' war is immensely painful.

BULLDOG ANT
Australia

The bulldog ant is a ferocious creature and is arguably the most lethal ant on the planet! It will repeatedly sink its venomous stinger in its victim while biting them with their huge, long-toothed mandibles.

GOLDEN POISON DART FROG
Columbia

FIERCE FACT:
THE INDIGENOUS EMBERÁ PEOPLE LACE THE TIPS OF THEIR BLOW DARTS WITH THE FROG'S POISON TO USE FOR HUNTING!

The golden poison frog is one of the most poisonous creatures on the planet. Just one small, two-inch frog has enough toxin in its skin to kill ten grown men.

BLACK MAMBA
Southern and Eastern Africa

FIERCE FACT:
WITHOUT BLACK MAMBA ANTIVENOM TREATMENT, THE BITE FROM THIS FEARSOME SNAKE IS 100% FATAL!

The black mamba is Africa's longest venomous snake and can grow up to 14 feet in length. This speedy serpent can slither as fast as 12.5 miles per hour. Because of its speed and potent venom, the black mamba is considered the deadliest of all snakes.

FIERCE FACT:

MALARIA SPREAD BY MOSQUITOS WAS ESTIMATED TO HAVE CAUSED 627,000 DEATHS IN 2020!

The little mosquito hardly seems deadly, but it is arguably the most dangerous animal in the world. The mosquito's bite can carry many diseases, including malaria— a widespread sickness affecting hundreds of millions of people annually.

PUFFERFISH
Tropical Oceans Worldwide

FIERCE FACT:
PUFFERFISH ARE THE SECOND MOST POISONOUS VERTEBRATE IN THE WORLD AND THEIR DEADLY TOXIN IS UP TO 1,200 TIMES MORE POISONOUS THAN CYANIDE!

In Japan, pufferfish are considered a delicacy and are prepared by specially trained, licensed chefs. They delicately remove the poisonous parts of the fish. Even then, every year, there are several accidental deaths from ingesting this toxic fish!

HIPPOPOTAMUS
Africa

This huge semi-aquatic animal is often considered the world's deadliest large land mammal. Not only that, but hippos are incredibly loud! Their booming grunts, snorts, and wheezes have been measured at 115 decibels which is as loud as standing near a speaker at a rock concert!

FIERCE FACT:
HIPPOS ARE EXTREMELY AGGRESSIVE, DANGEROUS GIANTS. THEY KILL APPROXIMATELY 500 PEOPLE A YEAR AND MAY ATTACK ANYTHING THAT WANDERS INTO THEIR TERRITORY!

DEATHSTALKER SCORPION

The Middle East, Africa, and Asia

FIERCE FACT:

THE DEATHSTALKER CAN DELIVER WHAT HAS BEEN DESCRIBED AS THE MOST PAINFUL STING IN THE WORLD!

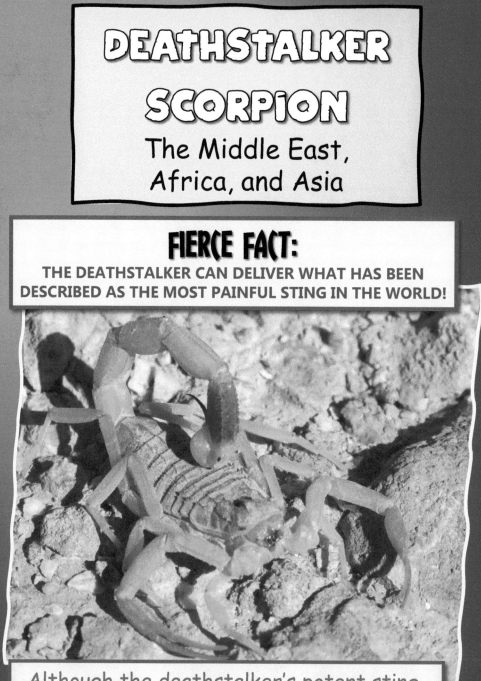

Although the deathstalker's potent sting is lethal, several of the toxins found in the venom are being used in medical research to help cancer patients!

BULL SHARK
Coastal Waters Across the World

FIERCE FACT:
BULL SHARKS TEND TO HEAD-BUTT THEIR PREY FIRST BEFORE ATTACKING THEM WITH THEIR SHARP, NEEDLE-LIKE TEETH!

Along with great white and tiger sharks, bull sharks are one of the three shark species most likely to attack humans. They can be found cruising the warm, shallow coastal waters in oceans worldwide. They are both aggressive and curious: a dangerous combination.

LION

Africa

African lions are fearless predators and
are often called kings of nature. They
are especially aggressive and dangerous
towards humans when protecting their
cubs, territory, or food.

ASIAN GIANT HORNET
Asia and North America

FIERCE FACT:
ASIAN GIANT HORNETS HAVE THE SCARY NICKNAME OF "MURDER HORNETS!"

The Asian giant hornet really is giant! Its stinger is 1/4 inch (6mm) long and delivers a potent venom that can be lethal. One scientist who was stung described the feeling as "like a hot nail being driven into my leg." Ouch!

INLAND TAIPAN
Australia

FIERCE FACT:
JUST ONE BITE FROM THE INLAND TAIPAN DELIVERS ENOUGH VENOM TO KILL 100 HUMAN ADULTS!

This Australian snake is a relative of the cobra and its venom is the most lethal in the world. Containing a mix of deadly toxins, this venom is fatal to warm-blooded animals.

WHY DOES AUSTRALIA HAVE SO MANY VENOMOUS SNAKES?

Australia is a beautiful country filled with many unusual and unique animals, but did you know it is also home to 20 of the 25 most venomous snakes in the world?

Some scientists explain that this may be due to the continental drift theory. Many years ago, the continents of the world were all joined together. This giant landmass gradually split apart, and over time the continents slowly drifted away from each other.

Before that happened, it is thought a venomous population of snakes lived in the region that would later become Australia. This snake family, called "elapids," are known for their short, hollow fangs that can inject neurotoxic venom. The diverse venomous snakes of Australia today are all descended from those original deadly ancestors.

Fortunately, many of these snakes live in desert regions far away from people. Most are shy creatures that avoid human contact. Australia also has plenty of "antivenom," a special medicine in case of a snakebite that counteracts the toxin. There are very few fatalities from snakes in Australia.

BLUE-SPOTTED STINGRAY
Indo-Pacific Oceans

FIERCE FACT:
THE TIP OF THE RAY'S TAIL HAS TWO VENOMOUS SPINES THAT CAN LASH OUT AND HIT A TARGET WITH BLINDING SPEED!

Although timid, these rays are very dangerous. The bright blue spots on the venomous ray's back serve as a warning to keep away. Their venom isn't usually fatal to humans, but their sting can cause horrible pain.

BLACK WIDOW
North America

The bright red marking on a black widow's abdomen is a striking identifier of this deadly arachnid! This spider's venom is 15 times stronger than that of a rattlesnake. Fortunately, their bite delivers just a tiny amount and there is an existing antivenom, so deaths from these spiders are rare.

HYENA
Africa

Despite their funny reputation, hyenas are no laughing matter. These creatures are larger and stronger than most people realize. They are adept killers who hunt both individually or as a pack.

FIERCE FACT:
HYENAS CAN RUN AS FAST AS 30 MILES PER HOUR AND ARE JUST AS DEADLY AS LIONS OR LEOPARDS!

FRESHWATER SNAIL

Across the World

FIERCE FACT:

THE WORLD HEALTH ORGANIZATION ESTIMATES THAT INFECTIONS FROM FRESHWATER SNAILS CAUSE 200,000 DEATHS A YEAR!

Who would've thought these tiny snails could be dangerous? It's true! They can carry one of the world's most dangerous parasitic diseases: schistosomiasis. Approximately 250 million people across the world are affected by this disease.

INDIAN COBRA
Indian Subcontinent

FIERCE FACT:
SOME INDIAN COBRAS CAN SPIT THEIR VENOM INTO A VICTIM'S EYES FROM SIX FEET AWAY!

These deadly venomous cobras are fearsome creatures. In the past, there were Indian performers known as "snake charmers" who would use these dangerous animals in their death-defying acts. This practice is outlawed in many places now, but some people still use these animals for show.

SALTWATER CROCODILE

Southeast Asia and Australia

These massive crocs can grow up to 23 feet in length and weigh over one ton! Not only are they the largest crocodile species in the world, but they are also the largest living reptile on the planet. Saltwater crocodiles are very aggressive and will attack a person if given a chance.

FIERCE FACT:
THE SALTWATER CROCODILE'S EXTREMELY POWERFUL JAWS GIVE THEM THE STRONGEST BITE OF ANY CREATURE IN THE ANIMAL WORLD!

SYDNEY FUNNEL-WEB SPIDER
Australia

These large Australian spiders have a bite so powerful their fangs can pierce fingernails. They build webs in the shapes of tunnels, where the spider sits and waits for their prey to touch the web.

STONEFISH
Indo-Pacific Ocean

FIERCE FACT:
A STING FROM THIS FISH CAN CAUSE EXCRUCIATING PAIN, RAPID SWELLING, PARALYSIS, AND EVEN DEATH!

The stonefish is a close relative to the scorpionfish and is the world's most venomous fish. They are masters at blending into their environment. The stonefish delivers their dangerous venom through a row of spines on its back if stepped on. With their natural camouflage, they often resemble coral or rocks as they rest motionless on the seafloor.

37

TSETSE FLY
Africa

The tsetse fly is the size of a large housefly and may not look very dangerous, but these biting flies can carry a serious disease called "sleeping sickness." The bite of the tsetse fly and the disease it spreads kills 275,000 people every year.

COMMON KRAIT

Indian Subcontinent

FIERCE FACT:
THE BITE OF THE KRAIT CAUSES LITTLE OR NO PAIN. BUT 4-8 HOURS LATER, THE NEUROTOXINS CAN CAUSE SUFFOCATION AND DEATH!

Also known as the "blue krait," this venomous snake is another one of the "Big Four" species that inflict the most snakebites on humans on the Indian subcontinent. The deadly bite of the krait causes more than 50% of the total snakebite deaths in Bangladesh.

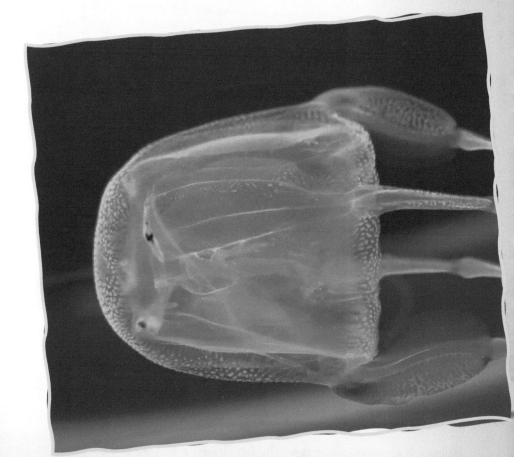

Box jellyfish are also known as "marine stingers" or "sea wasps." Up to 15 tentacles covered in thousands of stinging cells grow from the corners of their bell (body) and can reach 10 feet in length.

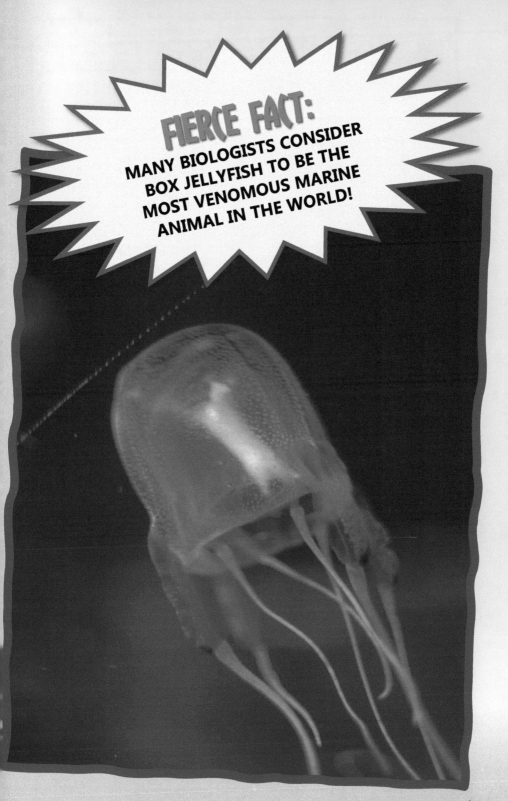

FIERCE FACT:
MANY BIOLOGISTS CONSIDER BOX JELLYFISH TO BE THE MOST VENOMOUS MARINE ANIMAL IN THE WORLD!

FAT-TAILED SCORPION
Northern Africa

Scorpions are part of the arachnid family and are closely related to spiders and ticks. The scientific genus name for this scorpion, Androctonus, translates from Greek to mean "man-killer."

DUCK-BILLED PLATYPUS
Australia

The platypus is one strange creature! They have a tail like a beaver, a furry body like an otter, and webbed feet like a duck. Male platypuses have sharp spurs on the back of their hind feet to stab and secrete venom. The venom is not fatal to humans, but the sting of a platypus causes severe swelling and excruciating pain.

43

GILA MONSTER
Southwestern U.S. and Mexico

Gila monsters are the largest lizards north of Mexico and are one of only two venomous lizards in the world. While the venom of the Gila monster isn't fatal to humans, their bites can be extremely painful. Fortunately, these lizards are mellow and won't bite unless provoked.

LIONFISH
Indo-Pacific Ocean and the U.S. Atlantic Coast

FIERCE FACT:
THE VENOMOUS STING OF A LIONFISH CAN LAST FOR DAYS AND CAUSE SWEATING, BREATHING PROBLEMS, EXTREME PAIN, AND EVEN PARALYSIS!

This invasive species of fish is spreading to many parts of the world. If someone is stung by the spines of a lionfish, the cure is to soak the wound in hot water. The heat helps break down the toxins.

ELEPHANT
Africa and Asia

Elephants are amazing animals who are very intelligent and can show emotions. Unfortunately, due to their strength and huge size, elephants occasionally kill people when scared or threatened, usually by trampling them. They can charge at up to 30 miles per hour.

FIERCE FACT:

A MALE AFRICAN ELEPHANT CAN WEIGH OVER 15,000 POUNDS AND ARE AS TALL AS 13 FEET AT THEIR SHOULDER!

BOOMSLANG

Africa

FIERCE FACT:
THE BOOMSLANG'S VENOM WILL CAUSE THE VICTIM TO BLEED TO DEATH INTERNALLY!

Boomslang means "tree snake" in Afrikaans and Dutch, so as you can imagine, this snake prefers to spend its time in trees. It is extremely agile and can climb trees and glide through tree branches while hunting.

BRAZILIAN
WANDERING SPIDER
Central and South America

Brazilian wandering spiders are a group of extremely venomous spiders found in Central and South America. They are the most venomous spiders in the world and spend their time wandering the jungle floor, looking for their next unlucky victim.

GREAT WHITE SHARK
Atlantic and Pacific Oceans

These sharks get their name from their bright white underbellies and are the largest predatory fish on Earth. With their streamlined bodies and powerful tails, they can cruise through water at speeds up to 15 miles per hour.

POLAR BEAR
The Arctic Circle

Although many people might think grizzlies are the most dangerous of all bears, that distinction goes to the polar bear. They are the largest of all bears, can outrun humans, and are immensely powerful. Unfortunately, the icy Arctic habitats where polar bears live are shrinking, leading to increased attacks on humans.

51

SOUTHERN CASSOWARY

Australia and Southeast Asia

Often called the world's most dangerous bird, the southern cassowary is large, aggressive, and fast. They're able to inflict massive damage with their razor-like claws and powerful kicks.

KISSING BUG

North, Central, and South America

FIERCE FACT:
SYMPTOMS FROM CHAGAS DISEASE GET PROGRESSIVELY WORSE OVER TIME AND CAN CAUSE DEATH 10-30 YEARS AFTER THE INITIAL INFECTION!

While it might have a sweet name, the kissing bug is only trouble! More than half of these insects carry a parasite that causes Chagas disease. The parasite is transmitted through the kissing bug's poop.

BLUE-RINGED OCTOPUS

Indo-Pacific Ocean

Don't let this cute little octopus fool you; they are dangerous when threatened! Although it isn't much bigger than an apple, this beautiful creature is one of the deadliest animals in the sea. One bite from their tiny beaks delivers enough toxic venom to paralyze a human in minutes.

FIERCE FACT:
THE BLUE-RINGED OCTOPUS PRODUCES THE SAME POTENT NEUROTOXIN FOUND IN PUFFERFISH!

EASTERN DIAMONDBACK RATTLESNAKE
North America

These huge, deadly snakes can strike as far as two-thirds of their body length. This means an 8-foot-long diamondback can strike a target over 5 feet away. Once they release their lethal venom, the snake will follow their prey until they die.

DEER TICK
North America

FIERCE FACT:
BECAUSE THE EARLY SYMPTOMS OFTEN RESEMBLE THE FLU, SCIENTISTS ESTIMATE THAT 90% OF LYME DISEASE INFECTIONS GO UNREPORTED!

This tiny arachnid can carry dangerous bacteria in its body. Once the blood-sucking tick attaches to their host, they transmit the bacteria which then turns into Lyme disease. Although Lyme disease isn't usually fatal, it will cause serious health problems that worsen over time.

TIGER
India and Western Asia

FIERCE FACT:

THE CHAMPAWAT TIGER, A BENGAL TIGRESS, WAS RESPONSIBLE FOR OVER 400 HUMAN DEATHS. SHE IS LISTED IN THE GUINNESS BOOK OF WORLD RECORDS FOR THE HIGHEST NUMBER OF FATALITIES FROM A TIGER!

Tigers are immensely muscular, carnivorous hunters. Due to these qualities and their unpredictable nature, experts rank tigers as the fifth most dangerous mammal in the world.

CORAL SNAKE
North America and Asia

FIERCE FACT:
SOME SNAKES HISS OR RATTLE WHEN THREATENED, BUT CORAL SNAKES FART TO SEND THEIR WARNINGS!

These small, vibrantly colored snakes look adorable but make no mistake, they are dangerous! Coral snakes have the second-strongest venom of any snake but don't have an effective bite due to the small size of their jaws and weak fangs.

AFRICANIZED
HONEYBEE
North, Central, and South America

Also known as "killer bees," these bees are actually an experiment gone wrong! In the 1950s, a scientist in Brazil was genetically modifying bees to increase honey production. The aggressive hybrid bees he created escaped into the wild and eventually migrated across the Americas.

KING COBRA
India and Southwest Asia

FIERCE FACT:
THE KING COBRA IS SO LARGE AND STRONG IT CAN LITERALLY "STAND UP" AND LOOK A FULL-GROWN PERSON IN THE EYE!

While this cobra doesn't have the most potent venom, a single bite can deliver enough neurotoxin to kill 20 people or even an elephant. In some countries like Vietnam, the king cobra is a protected species.

NILE CROCODILE
Africa

Fearless and ferocious, Nile crocodiles can grow up to 20 feet long and are responsible for hundreds of human deaths each year. This species easily wins the title of the most-dangerous crocodile in the world!

CANE TOAD
Australia

FIERCE FACT:
IN 1935, 102 CANE TOADS WERE BROUGHT TO AUSTRALIA TO CONTROL BEETLES DESTROYING SUGAR CANE FIELDS. TODAY THERE ARE OVER 200 MILLION CANE TOADS IN AUSTRALIA!

The invasive cane toad is becoming a big problem in some areas. Originally from Central and South America, they can now be found in other parts of the world. They excrete a milky-white toxin through their skin poisonous to humans and animals.

INDEX

Africanized Honeybee, 60,
    H. Briedenhann/Shutterstock.com
Asian Giant Hornet, 5, 25,
    Naoto Shinkai/Shutterstock.com
    David Carillet/Shutterstock.com
Australia, 27, TitoOnz/Shutterstock.com
Black Mamba, 17,
    NickEvansKZN/Shutterstock.com
Black Widow, 29, Sari ONeal/Shutterstock.com
Blue-Ringed Octopus, 54,55,
    Elena_photo_soul/Shutterstock.com
    Y. A. Rahman/Shutterstock.com
Blue-Spotted Stingray, 28,
    Krzysztof Odziomek/Shutterstock.com
Boomslang, 48, Stu Porter/Shutterstock.com
Box Jellyfish, 40, 41,
    Daleen Loest/Shutterstock.com
    Dewald Kirsten/Shutterstock.com
Brazilian Wandering Spider, 49,
    Martin Pelanek/Shutterstock.com
Brown Recluse, 10,
    Sari ONeal/Shutterstock.com
Bull Shark, 23,
    Carlos Grillo/Shutterstock.com
Bulldog Ant, 15, RugliG//Shutterstock.com
Cane Toad, 63, Mr. F/Shutterstock.com
Cape Buffalo, 8, Rudi Hulshof/Shutterstock.com
Common Krait, 39,
    Meet Poddar/Shutterstock.com
Cone Snail, 9, Laura Dts/Shutterstock.com
Coral Snake, 59,
    Patrick K. Campbell/Shutterstock.com
Deathstalker Scorpion, 22,
    Bens_Hikes/Shutterstock.com
Deer Tick, 57, KPixMining/Shutterstock.com
Duck-Billed Platypus, 43,
    Martin Pelanek/Shutterstock.com
Eastern Diamondback Rattlesnake, 56,
    Chase D'animulls/Shutterstock.com
Electric Eel, 7,
    Vladimir Wrangel/Shutterstock.com
Elephant, 46, 47,
    Frankandre/Shutterstock.com
    Daan de HvD/Shutterstock.com
Fat-Tailed Scorpion, 42,
    Ernie Cooper/Shutterstock.com
Freshwater Snail, 32,
    Natalia Sidorova/Shutterstock.com
Gila Monster, 44,
    Milan Zygmunt/Shutterstock.com

Golden Poison Dart Frog, 16,
    Thorsten Spoerlein/Shutterstock.com
Great White Shark, 50,
    Ramon Carretero/Shutterstock.com
Grizzly Bear, 12, 13,
    Dennis W Donohue/Shutterstock.com
Hippopotamus, 20, 21,
    PhotocechCZ/Shutterstock.com
    Josiane Boute/Pixabay.com
Hyena, 30, 31, J. Natayo/Shutterstock.com
    Ondrej Prosicky/Shutterstock.com
Indian Cobra, 33, Three Alienz/Shutterstock.com
Indian Saw-Scaled Viper, 3,
    D. Muthunayake/Shutterstock.com
Inland Taipan, 26, Ken Griffiths/Shutterstock.com
King Cobra, 61,
    Tb-photography/Shutterstock.com
Kissing Bug, 53, Neryxcom/Shutterstock.com
Komodo Dragon, 4,
    Gudkov Andrey/Shutterstock.com
Lionfish, 45, Dimakig/Shutterstock.com
Lion, 24, Four Oaks/Shutterstock.com
Man O' War, 14, Laurel A Egan/Shutterstock.com
Mosquito, 18, Frank60/Shutterstock.com
Nile Crocodile, 62, David Havel/Shutterstock.com
Polar Bear, 51, Pixabay.com
Pufferfish, 5, 19,
    Aristokrates/Shutterstock.com
    FtLaud/Shutterstock.com
Russell's Viper, 5, 11,
    Jaroslava V/Shutterstock.com
    Fabio Lotti/Shutterstock.com
Saltwater Crocodile, 34, 35,
    Susan Flashman/Shutterstock.com
    A. Machulskiy/Shutterstock.com
Southern Cassowary, 52,
    Matt Cornish/Shutterstock.com
    Fazwick/Shutterstock.com
Stonefish, 5, 37,
    Andy Deitsch/Shutterstock.com
    Y. Jitwattanatam/Shutterstock.com
Sydney Funnel-Web Spider, 36,
    Ken Griffiths/Shutterstock.com
Tiger, 58, JFS07/Shutterstock.com
Tsetse Fly, 38, Jaco Visser/Shutterstock.com

Enjoy these other great books by JACK LEWIS:

Never Bring a Zebracorn to School

Joy to the World: The Best Christmas Gift Ever

Wonderful World of Animals Series

Take a trip around the world to find the wildest, weirdest, and most adorable animals on the planet!

The Cutest Animals of the World

The Weirdest Animals of the World

Dangerous Animals of the World

Today I Found... Series

Magical children's stories of friendship and the power of imagination!

Today I Found a Unicorn

Today I Found a Mermaid

Today I Found an Elf

Fun with Family Series

A wonderful way to celebrate each special person in our families!

I Love My Mommy

Printed in the USA
CPSIA information can be obtained
at www.ICGtesting.com
LVHW070027151123
763986LV00020B/561